THE
FINANCIAL
CRASH

SIMON BATHURST

NEPPERHAN PRESS, LLC
YONKERS, NY

Published by Nepperhan Press, LLC
P.O. Box 1448, Yonkers, NY 10702
nepperhan@optonline.net
nepperhan.com

PUBLISHER'S NOTE
The opinions expressed and the conclusions drawn
in this analysis are those of the author.

Printed in the United States of America

ISBN 978-0-9794579-2-0

For the next generation

"At that moment we faced the fact that only the government could save the system."

Anonymous banker – September, 2008

CONTENTS

1

What happened?

It's getting dark, so you turn on a light—but nothing happens. You assume that the light-bulb is dead, so you replace it—but still nothing happens.

Then you look out the window and see that there are no lights in your neighbor's house. You go outside and look around and you see no lights anywhere. You conclude that the system that provides electricity has crashed.

You know there's nothing you can do about it, and you know how it'll affect you. Until they fix the problem you will have no light, no heat, no television. But you're confident that they will fix it, and meanwhile you can put up with it.

Thanks to all the media coverage, you know the financial system has crashed. You know there's nothing you can do about it, but you don't know how it'll affect you, and you're not confident that they will fix it because the people who are responsible for this system have no experience at fixing such problems. And maybe these people, for all their talk, don't even understand why it happened.

Politicians have easy answers—it happened because of greed on Wall Street. Yes, there was greed on Wall Street, but greed alone doesn't cause financial systems to crash. Other factors have to be present.

So why did the financial system crash? How will it affect you? And what should our government do to fix it?

Our dependence on credit

Most of us don't think about the financial system any more than we think about the system that provides electricity to our homes since we can almost always depend on these systems.

We know that if the power system crashes, we don't have electricity. But what happens when the financial system crashes? We don't have credit.

Credit is what we get from the financial system, just as we get electricity from the power system. And we all depend on credit—even if we're not using it directly.

Credit is a word with many meanings, but we can define its role in the financial system as an arrangement to defer payment for something which is based on trust.

When we buy a home we usually don't pay cash for it. We pay for it over many years, making monthly payments. This arrangement is a home mortgage.

When we buy a car we usually pay for it over several years, making monthly payments. This arrangement is a car loan.

When we buy a pair of shoes in a store we may use a credit card, which enables us to defer payment for our purchase. With this same arrangement we defer payment for a dinner in a restaurant or a trip to the Caribbean.

When we go to college or send our kids to college we may use a student loan to defer payment on the tuition and the room and board.

If you want to appreciate how much we depend on credit, imagine having to pay cash for everything, including your home and your car. You can see that if we *did* have to pay cash for everything, we wouldn't have things we have now.

A loss of trust

Going back to our definition of credit, we said that it's an arrangement to defer payment for something which is *based on trust*. That's very important.

When you use a mortgage to buy your home or a loan to buy your car or a credit card to buy furniture, you're using credit to defer payment, and someone is making a loan to you based on the assumption that you will repay it. That's where trust comes in. The lenders trust you to pay them back.

Why do they trust you with their money? Well, if you have a record of taking loans and not repaying them, they won't trust you—and they won't lend you any more money. But most of us have reasonably good credit histories, so lenders trust us based on those histories and based on current information about our ability to repay the loan.

If you think about it, you can see that lenders are making decisions about the future based on our past performance and our current potential. It's the same kind of process that sportswriters use in picking the likely winner of a football game or a tennis match. They look at past performance and current potential of teams and players.

We know that there are upsets in the sports world, so we shouldn't be surprised if there are wrong predictions in the financial world, but most of the time decisions by lenders to trust us with their money are well founded. In fact, lenders are right in their predictions far more often than sportswriters.

Imagine what would happen if lenders suddenly decided not to trust anyone. Since credit is always based on trust, then credit would suddenly stop flowing.

If you needed a mortgage, a car loan, or a credit card, you couldn't get it—no matter how good a credit history you had. It's like what happens when the power system crashes. No matter how faithfully you've paid your bills on time, you still have no electricity.

Since credit is what powers the financial system, and since credit is based on trust, then a sudden general loss of trust causes financial systems to crash.

At this point you might ask why there would be a sudden general loss of trust in the financial system.

To answer that question, we need to understand how the system works, we need to learn how banks and financial markets provide credit, and we need to track the events that led to a sudden general loss of trust.

So in the next several chapters we'll have a quick course on the financial system.

2

Banks

Most of us are familiar with banks, and we thought we knew what they were doing, but we were surprised to learn that they were doing things that even their highly paid executives didn't understand. But before we go into that, let's make sure we understand what banks were supposed to be doing.

The word "bank" is often used loosely, but for most of us it means those spiffy branches that have occupied the prime locations in our cities and suburbs, evidently because they can afford the rent. We use their cash machines, we may go into them to deposit checks or to request loans, and increasingly we use the services they make available online.

This type of bank is called a "commercial" bank because traditionally it was involved in commerce. But there are other types of banks, which don't have branches on the streets where we can see them. This type of bank is called an "investment" bank. And we need to talk about them too.

Commercial banks
Commercial banks make loans to individuals, including home mortgage loans, car loans, credit card loans, and student loans. They also make loans to businesses, governments, and other players in the financial system.

If you made a loan to your brother-in-law (which may not be advisable), you would dip into your pocket or your bank account and use your own money.

When a bank makes a loan it doesn't use its own money, it uses other people's money. It uses the money that we have on deposit in our checking accounts and savings accounts. And if the loan isn't repaid, the bank may not have enough money to return our money. But we trust banks with our money because it's insured by the government.

In the early 1930s thousands of banks failed because so many of their loans were not repaid, and people who had deposits with them lost their money. The widespread failure of banks and the total loss of savings were what made the Depression so severe. It's bad enough losing a third of your savings for retirement in the stock market, but imagine losing *all* your savings in a bank.

After that experience people didn't trust banks, so they didn't deposit their money with them, and without deposits the banks couldn't provide credit, and without credit the economy went into a tailspin.

To restore trust in the system the government created a system for insuring deposits up to a certain amount ($100,000 until recently), and if the bank couldn't return that money, the government would.

This system for insuring bank deposits is called the Federal Deposit Insurance Corporation (FDIC), and you'll probably see that acronym posted in your bank. If you don't see it, ask the bank manager and make sure that your account is insured by FDIC. If it's not, then take your money to a bank where your account *is* insured by FDIC.

In addition to taking deposits, commercial banks borrow money from the market, which enables them to make more loans than if they relied only on deposits. The money they borrow is typically due in ninety days or less. Repayment of this money is not covered by deposit insurance. It depends on trust. In other words, the lenders must have confidence that the banks are using their money wisely.

The important point to note is that companies that have more than the insured amount on deposit with a bank or have made loans to the bank could lose their money if the bank doesn't use it wisely. So unlike individuals, who generally don't have to worry about the bank, companies do have to worry about it, and if they hear a rumor about it, they'll take their money out of the bank.

Investment banks

Investment banks do not take deposits and make loans. The federal laws that were enacted following the crash of the financial system in 1929-32 made it illegal for investment banks to take deposits, with the idea that people's savings would not be exposed to the risks of investment banking.

Traditionally, investment banks arrange for companies to raise money by issuing securities. The banks underwrite the securities, meaning that they buy them from the companies and sell them to investors, making a profit on the difference between the price at which they buy and the price at which they sell the securities. If the companies fail, investment banks don't bear the risk.

In the case of loans, they have to convince investors that the companies can repay them, so they have to apply certain standards and maintain a certain level of quality. Investors make decisions based on the information provided by the investment banks. Though investment banks don't have to worry about losing their own money, they do have to worry about losing their reputation. If too many of their loans go bad, then investors won't do business with them.

In addition, federal and state laws require what we call "full disclosure" about the borrower. The information that the investment banks provide to the lenders must be accurate and complete. If they leave out the inconvenient fact that the business has lost its patent on the product that accounts for most of its revenues, they'll be in trouble with the law. So their traditional activities (arranging issues of stocks and bonds) are regulated by the government.

In recent years investment banks got more involved in direct lending, lured by the prospect of higher profits. Since they couldn't take deposits, they borrowed money in the market and used it to make loans. So they became dependent on the trust of lenders, just as commercial banks did.

Leverage

We hear the word "leverage" used in a variety of situations. It's an overused word, but it has a very particular meaning when we talk about banks.

Leverage is simply the extent to which a bank or any business uses other people's money in relation to its own money. And without qualification we can say that the higher the leverage, the riskier the situation.

A nonfinancial business might have one dollar of other people's money (borrowed money) for every dollar of its own money (capital). This money is invested in the means of providing a product or a service, and if the business starts losing money it has to lose half of its investment before the lenders are exposed to loss. The owners will lose a lot of money before the lenders lose any money.

A commercial bank might have ten dollars of other people's money (deposits and borrowed money) for every dollar of its own money (capital). So a commercial bank is much more highly leveraged than a typical nonfinancial business, which makes it riskier. Its money is mostly invested in loans, and if those loans start going bad, the bank only has to lose a tenth of its investment before the lenders are exposed to loss. The owners of a commercial bank will lose relatively little money before the lenders start losing money.

An investment bank might have twenty or even thirty dollars of other people's money (borrowed money) for every dollar of its own money (capital). So an investment bank is much, much more highly leveraged than a typical nonfinancial business, which makes it much, much riskier. Its money is mostly invested in securities, and if those securities start losing value, the bank only has to lose a twentieth (or a thirtieth) of its investment before the lenders are exposed to loss. The owners of an investment bank will lose very little money before the lenders start losing money.

How have commercial banks and investment banks gotten away with having such high leverage? Again, the answer is lenders trusted them to use the money wisely.

Of course they didn't always use the money wisely. If you look back at history you'll see that periodically banks got into trouble by going too far with some activity that looked like a sure winner. They collapsed, taking economies with them, and until the last century governments did nothing to protect people from the consequences of bankers gone wild. People just had to pick themselves up and start over again.

Why banks fail
There are two reasons why banks fail: they become illiquid or they become insolvent.

A bank becomes illiquid when it's no longer able to finance its loans with a source of money. In traditional banking the loans were financed by deposits, and banks became illiquid when too many of their depositors demanded the money that they had in checking accounts or savings accounts. Banks kept reserves of cash to meet such demands in normal times, but in situations where their depositors were panicking they almost never had enough cash to meet such demands because the deposits were mostly invested in loans, and banks can't demand payment on loans until they're due. And even then if the loans are bad they can't collect them.

The purpose of insuring bank deposits was to prevent people from panicking. If a bank fails, its depositors get their money from the government. So people with money in bank accounts that are covered by deposit insurance (as they are at most banks) no longer panic when they hear rumors about their bank or about the banking system.

But companies, banks, and other institutions that have made loans to a bank or have deposits in a bank in amounts that are greater than the limit on deposit insurance ($100,000 until recently) do panic when they hear rumors about their bank. And since they provide large amounts of money, a bank can become illiquid from one day to the next as its sources of borrowed money dry up.

At that point the bank could be worth saving if it doesn't have too many bad loans because eventually it'll collect the payments due on its loans and have enough money to pay its depositors and its lenders. But if it has so many bad loans that it won't have enough money to meet its obligations, then it becomes insolvent, and it's no longer in a position to operate as a going concern.

An important thing to understand is that if a bank becomes illiquid, it doesn't necessarily become insolvent. The problem is, while it's rather easy to determine if a bank is illiquid since everyone knows when a bank isn't able to meet the demands of its depositors or lenders, it's rather difficult to determine if a bank is insolvent since it takes time to find out if loans payable over several years are good or bad.

Winding down
When a bank takes losses, the amount of owner's money is reduced since the first losses go against this money. For example, if the bank had one dollar of owner's money (capital) for every ten dollars of other people's money (deposits and borrowed money), after taking losses it may now have only fifty cents of owner's money for the same amount of other people's money, which means that the latter are now more exposed to loss. Another way of saying this is that instead of

having a leverage of ten to one, the bank now has a leverage of twenty to one, so its situation is much riskier.

If lenders perceive the situation as much riskier, they are much less inclined to provide money to the bank, so they stop lending to it. At the same time depositors who are not fully covered by insurance withdraw their money.

The bank now doesn't have enough immediate funding to continue its business, and there are only two things it can do to restore what had been an acceptable leverage: it can raise more capital, or it can sell loans.

Since it's losing money, the bank is in a bad position to raise more capital. Why should anyone invest in it? And if anyone were interested, why not wait until the bank is in a worse position in order to get a better deal?

If the bank tries to sell loans, it'll have to mark them down significantly in order to induce someone to buy them, and that price, the marked-down price, will become the price at which the bank has to value similar loans that it still has on its books. So the bank will take more losses on its loans.

The bank is in a vicious cycle. It takes losses on its loans, which erode its capital and put its lenders more at risk. Its lenders stop providing money, and the bank now desperately needs funding. Its only recourse is to sell loans, which results in a further markdown in the value of the loans still on its books, which forces the bank to take more losses, and so on, until the bank collapses.

Meanwhile, the bank is not making any new loans, and if a lot of other banks are in this situation, we have what's called a "credit crunch." The banks have stopped making new loans. The financial system has crashed.

If banks hadn't been so highly leveraged to begin with, they would have had a bigger cushion against loan losses, and it would have taken longer for the system to crash, or the system might never have crashed. So what degree of leverage would have prevented the system from crashing?

That depends on what banks are doing with other people's money. If they stick to making traditional loans with high standards for evaluating the borrower's ability to repay, and if they rely almost entirely on a lot of small deposits as a source of money, then a ten-to-one leverage might be appropriate.

But if banks venture into other areas where the risk is hard to evaluate, and if they rely to a great extent on borrowed money, then they should have a lower leverage.

Where do banks get borrowed money? They get it from financial markets. And to understand these markets, we have to know something about securities.

3

Securities

The word "security" means freedom from danger, fear, or anxiety. It produces positive feelings since it appeals to a basic human need.

In the field of finance the word means an evidence of debt or ownership. Traditionally, securities were pieces of paper with signatures and seals on them. Now they're more likely to be entries in a data system.

Securities play a major role in the financial system, so we need to know the basic types of securities that are traded in financial markets.

Types of securities

Common stock is evidence of ownership. It gives you a share of a business, which is why stocks are called "shares," and it usually gives you voting rights.

The company issuing the stock does not promise anything other than to treat you like every other common shareholder. It has no obligation to pay you money at any time, though from time to time it may voluntarily pay you a share of its earnings (dividends).

To acquire common shares you have to buy them from someone, and the only way you can get your money back is to sell them to someone. The company that issued the shares is not obligated to buy them back, though from time to time it may offer to buy back its shares.

Common stock is very risky. If a company goes out of business the common stockholders (the owners) are first in line to lose their money.

Preferred stock does not give you a share of a business and usually does not give you voting rights.

The company issuing preferred stock agrees to pay you a rate of return, which is called a dividend, but it has no relation to earnings. If the company does well, you have no benefit, but your dividends have priority over the dividends on common stock, and if a company goes out of business the common shareholders will lose their money before you do.

Preferred stock is slightly less risky than common stock, but it's still risky.

A bond is evidence of debt. The word has the meaning of being tied or bound by something, so a bond is a binding agreement by the borrower to repay the lender.

In a typical bond the borrower pays a fixed rate of interest to the lender every six months over a period of twenty years, and then at the end of that period repays the original amount of the loan (the principal).

Bondholders do not have a share of the business, nor do they have voting rights under normal circumstances, but if the company goes out of business they have the right to be paid before preferred or common stockholders.

Bonds are less risky than common or preferred stock, but they are still risky—how risky depends on the borrower.

If the borrower is the U.S. Treasury, we usually assume that the lender has no risk of nonpayment (default), but if the borrower is a company with potential problems then its bonds can be very risky, and depending on your point of view they are "high-yield" bonds or "junk" bonds.

This raises an important point. The higher the risk of default on a bond, the higher interest rate it has to pay since lenders want to be rewarded for taking a higher risk.

At the shorter end there are a variety of debt securities that obligate the borrower to repay the loan in a year or less. They are called "money market instruments," and they are the securities found in money market mutual funds.

The standard security in the money market is the U.S. Treasury bill, an obligation of the Federal government to repay the lender. Treasury bills can have due dates (maturities) of up to one year, but most Treasury bills are due in six months or less. As with Treasury bonds, we assume there is no risk of default since unlike all other borrowers the Federal government if necessary can raise taxes or print money to pay its obligations.

Another security in the money market is commercial paper, an obligation of a corporation to repay the lender. Like the Treasury bill, commercial paper is a simple promise to pay an amount at maturity, and most commercial paper is due in three months or less. Unlike the Treasury bill, commercial paper has risk of default, so companies pay higher rates than the Treasury, but only those companies that are regarded as creditworthy are able to sell their paper in the market, so the risk (under normal circumstances) is relatively low.

The bank CD, a security in the money market, should not be confused with certificates of deposit that individuals have with banks (nor with the disks on which music is recorded). The bank CD is an obligation of a bank to pay the lender principal plus interest at maturity, and most bank CDs are due in three months or less. As with commercial paper, there is risk of default, so banks pay higher rates than the Treasury, though until recently the risk of banks defaulting on their CDs was considered to be relatively low.

There is one remaining security in the money market that we need to talk about, though it doesn't look like a security. It's an obligation that arises when one bank borrows from another bank. The loans from one bank to another are for short maturities, usually overnight, but they play an important role in enabling banks to remain liquid and meet requirements of the Federal Reserve (our central bank).

These loans are called "Fed funds," which is misleading since it implies that the banks are borrowing from the Federal Reserve when in reality they are borrowing from other banks. The justification for calling them Fed funds is that the rate for such loans is determined by the Federal Reserve, which uses this rate as an economic tool.

When a bank makes a loan to another bank there is no piece of paper or electronic entry that can be traded in a market, so in that sense Fed funds are different from all the other securities we've talked about. In other words, if you've made a loan to another bank you can't unload it in the market, you're stuck with it.

Liquidity

If something is marketable that means it can be easily sold in a market for "used" items (a secondary market). For example, a stock listed on the New York Stock Exchange can be easily sold in that market. Some bonds, such as Treasury bonds and high-grade corporate bonds, can be easily sold, but not all stocks and bonds can be easily sold.

Suppose your brother-in-law starts a business and sets up a corporation and issues shares. He may offer to pay for your services by giving you shares of this corporation, but watch out—these shares aren't marketable, so they can't be easily sold. In fact, you might end up using them to start fires or to cover the floor when you paint.

We already talked about banks failing when they become illiquid, so now it would be useful to extend the concept of liquidity to assets. An asset is something you own, like a house or a car or a bond, and the easier it is to turn the asset into cash without a significant markdown in its price, the more liquid it is. The standard for measuring liquidity is cash, so we can say that cash is a perfectly liquid asset. Cash in the bank is almost perfectly liquid, though we can't produce this cash by simply opening our wallet.

Certain types of marketable securities are very liquid. For example, Treasury bills can be turned into cash within a day or two, depending on your situation. Treasury bills are very liquid for several reasons. First, they're obligations of the Federal government, so we have no doubt about whether or when the borrower will pay. Second, Treasury bills are short-term, and (other things being equal) the shorter the term of a debt security, the more liquid it is. And third, Treasury bills are traded in a very large volume, and (other things being equal) the higher the volume in which a security is traded, the more liquid it is. So Treasury bills are a standard against which we measure the liquidity of other securities.

Other types of short-term debt security are less liquid than Treasury bills because there is risk of nonpayment, however slight, and they are traded in lower volumes. For example, commercial paper is less liquid than Treasury bills for those two reasons, and so are bank CDs. But in normal times they can be easily sold in the market.

Fed funds are not liquid because they're not traded in a secondary market. They're usually due the next day, but if you want your money back today you have to borrow it from someone. And what happens if at that time no one is willing to lend to you?

4

Financial markets

A market is a place or a system for exchanging one thing for another. Many people go to farmers' markets where they buy fresh produce and organic chicken and homemade pasta and whole-grain breads and other such things. They exchange their money for the products.

In these markets the sellers usually set the prices, and the buyers accept them or else they don't buy. In livelier markets there is haggling over prices, with buyer and seller each giving ground and finally meeting somewhere in the middle.

If an exchange takes place, then we can assume that the price is right for buyer and seller. We say that this price is the one that presently "clears" the market.

The principles that apply to farmers' markets apply as well to financial markets, though most people have more trouble understanding financial markets, maybe because you can't prepare a dinner with what you buy there, and you can't touch or smell what you bought.

But if we remember that markets are only places or systems for exchanging one thing for another, then we should have no trouble understanding financial markets. So let's begin with two types of financial market: exchange markets and over-the-counter markets. Though they perform the same functions, they operate in very different ways.

Exchange markets

An exchange market is a place where people offer to buy or sell something at prices that they believe are appropriate.

Let's use the New York Stock Exchange as an example since most of us have heard of it. To trade on this exchange you have to be a member, so it's like a club in that respect. It doesn't let just anyone come in and trade.

Its purpose is to trade shares of businesses that confer the holders with the risks and rewards of ownership.

To buy or sell shares you have to use a licensed broker, and you have to demonstrate that within the limits of your trading you're good for the money.

If you weren't good for the money and you agreed to buy one hundred shares of a company at $50 per share, and if you couldn't pay for the shares, the seller (who thought she had a deal) would be exposed to the risk of having to sell the next day at a lower price.

So there are rules and regulations, not to mention laws, which ensure that the New York Stock Exchange operates smoothly. Of course the rules and regulations and laws don't prevent the prices of stocks from going down, but they do ensure that this market keeps functioning.

The key thing to understand about an exchange market is that the prices are set by buyers and sellers, not by some arbitrary mechanism, and the price of a stock is the latest price at which a transaction occurred.

Suppose you call your broker and offer to sell your one hundred shares of Company X at $50 per share. Your offer to sell goes to the exchange, where there might be an offer to buy one hundred shares of Company X at $47 per share. At that point there's no transaction since the seller's price and the buyer's price do not match.

Your broker might call you and tell you that there's no deal at $50 per share but there might be a deal at $49. You authorize your broker to sell at $49, and meanwhile the buyer might have authorized her broker to buy at $48.

There's still no match, but eventually if you and the buyer meet at $48.50 then there will be a deal.

Let's note some key points about this type of market.

First, your relationship with your broker is based on trust. A cynic might tell you not to trust your broker, and he could make some arguments to that effect, but the broker's behavior (unlike the cynic's) is governed by rules and regulations.

Second, an exchange market is transparent, so you can see the prices and volumes at which the shares of Company X traded during that day. You might not have sold at the highest price, but you know if you were in the ballpark.

Let's remember that we're talking about the stock market, which since the 1930s has been highly regulated in order to protect ordinary individuals. Other exchange markets, where ordinary individuals are less likely to do business, are not so regulated, though they have rules that govern behavior and provide transparency.

Over-the-counter markets

The phrase "over the counter" suggests that business is being done between two people standing on opposite sides of a counter, as when you go into a bank and make a deposit. That may be what used to happen in these markets, but "over the counter" now means that transactions to buy and sell are not done in a physical location, they are done over the phone or through electronic systems.

Since most over-the-counter markets are dealer markets, we need to understand what dealers do. Unlike brokers, who simply arrange transactions between buyers and sellers, dealers buy and sell for their own accounts.

The people who sell us cars are dealers since they buy the cars from manufacturers or previous owners and then try to sell them, whereas the people who help us buy a home are brokers since they arrange for us to buy the home from the owner but do not buy it and then try to sell it.

Dealers make money by selling something at a higher price than they paid for it, whereas brokers make money from the commissions they charge for their services.

By the nature of their operations, dealers take a bigger risk than brokers since whatever they buy for their own account they could end up selling at a loss, whereas brokers are never in that position. The worst that can happen to brokers is that they don't earn any commissions.

In over-the-counter markets the transactions are usually done through dealers, with brokers directing customers to them. For example, in the Nasdaq market dealers buy stocks at one price, sell them at another price, and usually make a profit on the difference between these prices.

Dealers post the prices at which they are willing to buy and sell, so this type of market is transparent in that you can determine the value of a particular stock by looking at the prices posted by dealers.

If you want to buy shares of Company Y, which are traded in a dealer market, you ask your broker to get you a price, which she will get from a firm that makes a market in these shares. She will get the price at which the dealer is willing to sell, and if you're happy with that price you'll buy the shares. If not, you'll ask your broker to try to get the shares at a lower price, which she may or may not be able to do.

Of course a dealer's prices must be responsive to the ultimate buyers or sellers of stock—if the price at which a dealer is willing to buy is too low, then no one will sell to him. So in their own way dealer markets fulfill the same function as exchange markets of enabling people to trade shares at prices that reflect their market value.

Remember, the price at which the dealer is willing to sell the shares is based on the price at which he bought them, and it'll be a bit higher—unless the dealer has decided to unload the shares as soon as possible.

The main difference between the two types of market is that in over-the-counter markets securities are bought and sold by dealers, whereas in exchange markets they are bought and sold by investors.

In markets for securities that ordinary people trade (stocks and bonds), both types of market are highly regulated, so they are equally reliable. But in markets that are less regulated, the over-the-counter type of market presents more risks and is more prone to failure than the exchange type of market, for reasons that we shall see in the following pages.

Standardization of securities

In explaining the two different types of market we used the example of stock markets since they're the ones that people are most familiar with. Stock markets get a lot of coverage in the media, whereas other markets may get no coverage unless something goes wrong.

Stocks can be traded in exchange markets or over the counter, and so can bonds, though most bonds are traded over the counter. Two factors that determine whether a stock or a bond is traded on an exchange are the size of the company and the volume available for trading. If there isn't much volume of a security available for trading, then it's not worthwhile for an exchange to list that security.

Another key factor that determines whether securities are traded on an exchange is their degree of standardization. For example, one common share of Company X is the same as every other common share of that company, so this security is highly standardized. Or if the company issues bonds that are due in 2028 with a fixed interest rate, then every $1,000 of those bonds is the same as every other $1,000 of those bonds, so this security is highly standardized.

With standardization, trading is greatly simplified. You only have to know how many units people want to buy or sell at a given time, and since the units are interchangeable, you can get some here and others there without having to pick and choose among them. You can aggregate these standardized securities from any source.

But if securities are customized they're difficult to trade on exchanges, which depend on standardization. In the extreme case, a security that's one of a kind is difficult to trade in any type of market. We can also say that about a security that's hard for most people to understand.

Between common stocks or simple bonds at one extreme and highly customized or very arcane securities at the other extreme, there are types of securities that can be standardized and therefore can be easily traded on exchanges. We'll look at those types of securities later when we talk about hedging and speculating.

Market failure

A market fails when it becomes impossible to sell a given type of security in that market at any price. Such failure could occur in both exchange markets and over-the-counter markets, but it's less likely to occur in an exchange market.

A company listed on a stock exchange can fail, and prices of all listed stocks can decline to abysmal levels, but the market doesn't fail. It's still possible to sell stocks at some price, and that's because exchanges operate through a process of matching prices of buyers and sellers, not through a process of buying stocks for their own accounts and then reselling them. Exchange markets don't buy securities, so they don't get stuck with big positions of securities that they can't sell.

But dealers, on which over-the-counter markets depend, *do* get stuck with big positions of securities that they can't sell. For example, if a dealer is left holding commercial paper issued by a company that just went bankrupt, he might not be able to sell it, and if there's a panic, dealers might not be able to sell commercial paper issued by any company at any price. So the market for commercial paper could fail.

If this type of seizure could occur in the commercial paper market, a long-established market for a simple, standardized security, imagine what could happen in relatively new markets for complex, customized securities.

5

Banks and financial markets

Banks and financial markets are the main components of the financial system, and all other components of the system relate to them in one way or another.

The difference between them is that banks take deposits and borrow from those who have excess money and lend it to people who need money. In other words, banks facilitate an *indirect* flow of funds from lenders to borrowers.

Since banks stand between the two parties, the people who deposit money in a bank or lend money to a bank are looking to the bank to return their money when they want it back. They're not looking to the people the bank made loans to, though of course if the bank makes a lot of bad loans, some depositors and lenders might not get all their money back, so they have a stake in the quality of the bank's loans, whether or not they know it.

Markets facilitate a *direct* flow of funds between buyers and sellers or between lenders and borrowers without standing between the two parties, so if the stock goes down or the loan goes bad, the markets themselves don't lose money. Dealers can lose money if between the time they buy a security and the time they resell it the value of the security goes down, but traditionally they minimized this risk by not holding securities any longer than necessary.

Though they perform different functions in the financial system, banks and markets need each other, and in recent years their relationship of mutual dependence has become so close that it's sometimes hard to tell them apart.

How banks depend on markets

A generation ago banks used markets for two main things. They held marketable securities such as Treasury bills as a secondary reserve in case they needed cash to meet demands from depositors. In other words, they used financial markets as a source of extra liquidity.

Banks also used financial markets as a means of making some extra profits from trading securities. Banks acted as dealers in securities that governments and corporations issued to borrow money short term. As dealers, they posted prices at which they would buy and sell these securities, and they made profits (most of the time) on the difference between these two prices. They also did some speculation in this area, though not too much at that time.

Then came a revolution in banking. Until then the amount of loans that a bank could make was limited by the amount of its deposits, which in turn were limited by geography and by banking regulations. It occurred to some banks that they could make a lot more loans if in addition to taking deposits they borrowed money in the market, as the government and large corporations did.

So they invented a security called a bank CD that enabled corporations that had temporary excess money to earn interest on that money just as they could on Treasury bills, except that the rate would be somewhat higher. The banks got dealers, including their own, to make a market in CDs so that the corporations that held them could sell them at any time if they needed their money back.

With the invention of the CD as a new source of funding, banks could make more loans, and they looked virtually everywhere for lending opportunities, which inevitably got them into trouble because when banks can make more loans they always make more bad loans.

As banks expanded using borrowed money, they had to keep borrowing money, which they did by issuing new CDs to pay off the old ones when they came due (rolling them over), and as they kept expanding, they had to borrow more and more money just as the Treasury did (and still does), except that banks don't have the Treasury's power to collect taxes or print money to repay their debt.

The banks' new dependence on borrowed money exposed them to a new type of liquidity risk. If they heard a rumor about their bank, the corporations on which it depended for borrowed money might suddenly decide to stop lending to it. Remember, deposits were insured only up to $100,000, and bank CDs were typically issued in multiples of $1 million, so the corporations that loaned money to banks were virtually not covered by insurance. The money the bank had borrowed in the market was tied up in loans that didn't come due for several years, so if the bank was unable to roll over its CDs, it became illiquid and it failed. That happened to a number of banks in the early 1980s, and for a while it looked as if they had learned their lesson.

How markets depend on banks

Traditionally, markets depended more on banks than the other way around since banks were a primary source of funds that enabled dealers to buy securities and hold them for a short time instead of having to sell them immediately.

There are two main reasons why dealers would want the ability to hold securities. First, if the dealer is buying newly issued stocks or bonds from a corporation, he may want to sell them over a period of several days instead of dumping them all at once. If he can release the new securities into the market at a measured pace, then usually he'll be able to sell them at a higher price and make a bigger profit. So the dealer borrows from a bank to carry the unsold securities until the next day, pledging the securities as collateral, and he may continue borrowing over the next few days in declining amounts as he works down his inventory.

Another reason why a dealer would want to hold securities is if he believes that their price will rise. In this situation, he's taking a position (speculating). If he's right about the price going up, then he'll make a profit from his speculation. If he's wrong, he'll lose money. Again, he'll pledge the securities as collateral for a bank loan, so what he's doing looks the same as if he were borrowing to carry the securities for a short time before selling them. But it's not the same. He's betting on the future value of the securities, so what he's doing is riskier than holding a temporary inventory.

To finance their positions, some dealers were able to borrow from the market by issuing their paper, provided that they had a backup line of credit from a bank. These backup lines were required in case of market failure of the type we talked about earlier, when it becomes impossible to sell a type of security (in this case commercial paper) at any price. For banks, providing backup lines was good business since they collected fees for making the lines available, believing that they would never be used.

In recent years dealers have been acting more and more like banks by investing their capital and borrowed money in securities in which they were taking positions. Like banks they made a profit from the difference between the rate of interest they were earning on the securities they held and the rate of interest they were paying for the money they borrowed. So it paid for them to take positions, but their positions, especially in long-term debt securities, exposed them to risks that were much higher than the risks they would have normally incurred from buying and selling securities.

Turning loans into securities

When people talk about innovation in the financial system, one of the things they have in mind is the way banks found ways to turn their loans into securities (securitization).

It started years ago with home mortgage loans, which are loans from banks to individuals that enable the latter to buy homes. These loans are payable over periods of fifteen to thirty years, but unlike the bonds we talked about they require monthly payments of principal along with the interest. So the borrower is gradually paying down the principal over the life of the loan, though during the first ten years of a mortgage the borrower is mainly paying interest.

Which raises an important point. Though people who buy homes using a mortgage are referred to as "homeowners," they really don't own the home until they have paid off their mortgage, and it takes a lot of payments before they have a significant share of ownership (equity) in the home. Until late in the mortgage the bank has a lot more at stake.

Traditionally, banks that made home mortgage loans kept them on their books, so it took them a long time to recover the money they invested in such loans. In the meantime they couldn't make more loans with this money since it was tied up in mortgage loans. Then someone came up with an idea that enabled banks to sell these loans to the market and recover their money right away.

In fact, the government came up with the idea. Wanting to promote home ownership but realizing that banks had limited capacity to make mortgage loans, the government helped to create a market for "used" home mortgages (a secondary market). This market could tap into sources of funding that weren't directly available to banks, which greatly expanded their capacity to make mortgage loans. Instead of keeping these loans on their books, they could sell them to the market, recover their money, and make new loans.

When a bank closes a mortgage loan it collects a fee, which is a profit. If the bank holds the mortgage over thirty years, it has to spread this profit over that period, but if it sells the mortgage after the closing, it can take this profit all at once. So a bank has a profit motive for selling old loans as quickly as possible and making new ones.

To create a market for "used" home mortgage loans, the government sponsored two new institutions, Fannie Mae and Freddie Mac, whose purpose was to buy these loans from the banks that originated them. A typical bank had hundreds of such loans on its books, which if they met certain standards could be batched together and sold in a package.

Fannie Mae bought these packages and then used them to create debt securities that could be sold in the market to investors. The securities were backed by a batch of mortgages, which provided a stream of monthly payments to repay the investors who had bought them. The ultimate source of these payments came from the people who had borrowed from the banks to buy homes. So these securities were considered to have a low risk since everyone knew that people would always pay their mortgages.

At that time the percentage of people who failed to pay their mortgages (default rate) was very low since banks made sure that borrowers met certain credit standards. For example, the borrower was required to make a down payment on the home of ten to twenty percent. The down payment gave the borrower ownership (equity) in the home or something to lose by not paying the mortgage. The borrower's having an equity position helped keep the default rate low.

The down payment also reduced the bank's risk in the event that the borrower defaulted and the bank had to sell the home. Since the loan was for eighty to ninety percent of what the borrower paid for the home, the bank could sell the home for less and still recover all its money.

Another credit standard was the limit on the amount that a bank would lend in relation to the borrower's income. Before you were approved for a loan, you had to provide verification of your income, and then the bank limited the loan to a certain percentage of your income. You couldn't get a loan above that limit, so you either had to make a larger down payment or find a home with a lower price. In other words, you couldn't get a mortgage loan that you would be unable to pay.

Then things changed. As the prices of homes kept going up, people began to believe that they would always go up, and banks began to relax their standards. For example, if you bought a home with no down payment, in a few years you would have equity in the home because its price would go up. Since our economy was prospering, it was safe to assume that everyone could earn enough income to pay a mortgage, so it wasn't necessary to verify the borrower's income or to limit the amount of the loan to a certain percentage of that income. That was just a waste of time.

For bankers the reasoning was simple. The more mortgage loans they originated and the faster they turned these loans over, the more fees they would collect and the higher the bonuses they would receive.

It was a no brainer.

6

Spreading risk

The time has come to talk about securities that were designed to protect businesses from various risks. These securities are known as "derivatives" since their values are derived from the underlying values of commodities, stocks, bonds, currencies, and so on. But don't let that word put you off. If we look at a few types of derivative, which have their own names, you'll find them easy to understand, and you'll wonder what all the fuss was about.

Commodity futures

Let's start with commodity futures, which they say go back to the time of the Babylonians. Their purpose is to protect producers and users of a commodity such as wheat from adverse changes in its price.

Suppose you're a farmer with fields of wheat that you expect to harvest in three months. For you an adverse change would be for the price of wheat to go down and be lower when you sell your crop than it is now. So how do you protect yourself? You sell your wheat now for delivery at the time when you expect to harvest it, and you fix the price now, so that if the price of wheat goes down between now and then, you'll still get that fixed price. In this way you can insure yourself against the risk of an adverse change in price. We call this action "hedging," and we call the security that you use a "futures contract."

Who would agree to fix a price now on wheat that will be delivered three months from now? A flour mill that will need wheat at that time. For the flour mill an adverse change would be for the price of wheat to go up, or the opposite of what the farmer is worried about. And that's what makes a futures market possible—people worry about opposite things.

So while the farmer uses a futures contract to fix the price of wheat that he'll *sell* in three months, the flour mill uses a futures contract to fix the price of wheat that it'll *buy* at that time. The farmer and the flour mill are on opposite sides of the same contract, with one selling wheat and the other buying it, both of them fixing the price now for a future delivery to protect themselves from an adverse change.

At this point we should mention that the people using the futures market aren't all hedging (protecting themselves from an adverse change in price). Some of them may be speculating, or betting on the price of wheat. Politicians say that's not good, and they blame a lot of problems on speculators, but remember that when the farmer wants to hedge his risk there may not be a flour mill ready to take the other side, so having speculators ready to do that helps the hedgers. In other words, it broadens the market and makes the hedging more efficient (less costly).

We should also mention that commodity futures operate through exchange markets. The contracts are standardized and therefore are interchangeable, which makes them marketable. As we said earlier, this type of market puts buyers and sellers together at prices that are acceptable to both parties. And there are rules of the game that prevent the parties from not complying with their obligations.

These rules are similar to those of poker, which has recently become popular on television. If two people are playing poker, they both have to "ante" or put some money on the table before each hand. The ante guarantees that if a person drops out of the hand because he doesn't like his cards, there will be some money to pay the winner.

In a similar way the two parties to a futures contract have to provide money (margin) to the exchange to cover the risk of their dropping out because they don't like the direction of the change in price.

But here's where the rules of the exchange are different from the rules of poker. As the price begins to go against one of the parties the exchange requires him to put up more money (more margin), and if he doesn't the exchange finds another party to take his place. That's easy to do because the exchange still has more than enough money from the original party to cover the contract's decline in value, so it can sell the contract at a lower price. The new party to the contract has to put up money at that time, so there's always a party on the other side of the contract who is good for the money.

Why does the other party have to be good for the money? Because, as in a two-person game of poker, there is a winner on the futures contract and there is a loser. If the price of wheat goes down, the farmer who contracted to sell wheat at a fixed price in three months will win because he has the right to sell at a higher price than the market price at the time of delivery. The exchange pays the farmer the money he has won, and that offsets the lower price he receives for the wheat he sells in the real market. He has no net gain but no net loss, so the futures contract has protected him against an adverse change in price.

What about the flour mill? Though the price of wheat has gone down, the flour mill is obligated to buy wheat at a higher price than the market price at the time of delivery, so the flour mill has lost money on the futures contract. But this loss is offset by the fact that the flour mill can now buy wheat in the real market at a lower price than it would have paid when it entered into the futures contract. The flour mill has no net loss but no net gain, and during the three-month period the futures contract has protected it against an adverse change in price, which could have gone the other way.

The most important point is that in an exchange market there's no risk of the other party defaulting on its obligations, which we call "counterparty risk." No matter which party loses on the contract, the exchange always has enough money to pay the winner. That's why futures markets that operate on exchanges don't fail.

Financial futures

Financial futures function in the same way as commodity futures, which is no accident since the former were modeled after the latter.

Financial futures are relatively new, but sooner or later someone was going to figure out that if you could protect businesses from adverse changes in the prices of commodities, you could use the same system to protect businesses from adverse changes in the price of money (interest rates).

Suppose that three months from now the manager of an investment fund expects to receive a large amount of money, which he plans to invest in bonds. What should he worry about? He should worry that interest rates on bonds will be lower in three months than they are now, so the fund will earn a lower rate on its investment.

How can he protect the fund against this risk? He can buy a futures contract on Treasury bonds for delivery in three months. The Treasury bonds under the contract should be for the same amount and have the same maturities as the bonds in which he plans to invest.

On the other side of the contract is the treasurer of a corporation who plans to borrow a large amount of money in three months by issuing (selling) bonds in the market. What should she worry about? She should worry that interest rates on bonds will be higher in three months than they are now, so the corporation will have to pay a higher rate on its bonds.

How can she protect the corporation against this risk? She can sell a futures contract on Treasury bonds for delivery in three months. The Treasury bonds under the contract should be for the same amount and have the same maturities as the bonds that she plans to issue.

Now, neither of these people is going to do anything with Treasury bonds. The interest rate on Treasury bonds, which other bonds track, will simply determine who wins and who loses on the contract.

If interest rates go down, the fund manager who contracted to buy Treasury bonds for delivery in three months will win because when interest rates on bonds go down their prices go up, so he has the right to buy Treasury bonds at a lower price than the market price at the time of delivery. The exchange pays him the money he won, and that offsets the lower rate the fund will earn on the bonds that it buys in the real market. He has no net gain but no net loss, so the futures contract has protected him against an adverse change in interest rates.

What about the corporate treasurer? Since interest rates on bonds have gone down (and their prices have gone up), the corporation is obligated to sell Treasury bonds at a lower price than the market price at the time of delivery, which means that the corporation has lost money on the futures contract. But this loss is offset by the fact that the corporation can now issue bonds in the real market at a lower interest rate than it would have paid when it entered into the futures contract. The corporation has no net loss but no net gain, and during the three-month period the futures contract has protected it against an adverse change in interest rates, which could have gone the other way.

Like commodity futures, financial futures are traded in exchange markets, so there's no counterparty risk. No matter which party loses on the contract, the exchange always has enough money to pay the winner.

New ways of hedging

The methods of hedging we have talked about worked fairly well over time, but there were risks that they didn't cover, so people came up with some new ways of hedging.

We'll focus on the risk of nonpayment (default risk), which we've talked about before. In traditional banking default risk was heavily concentrated in commercial banks, which made loans and kept them on their books.

When banks began to turn their loans into securities that could be sold in the market, they began to spread the default risk. For example, instead of banks bearing the default risk on home mortgage loans, investors began to bear this risk, and as more and more loans were generated for sale to the market, the more this risk was spread to investors.

But banks still had to worry about default risk on the loans they kept on their books and the loans they bought from other banks, so they invented a security that would protect them against this risk. It was called a "credit default swap."

In a typical transaction (if there was such a thing), a bank would buy insurance from another institution to protect itself against default risk in a particular situation. For example, a bank might start to worry about default on a loan it had made to a particular company, and not being able to sell the loan, it would insure the loan against default by paying money to another party, which was willing (and presumably able) to bear the risk. After buying the insurance the bank stopped worrying about the loan, and it then made other risky loans, believing it could always insure them.

Though the bank had protected itself against default risk, it now had counterparty risk—the risk that the party that had sold it the insurance wouldn't be good for the money. Which looks like default risk in another guise.

Meanwhile, that party would buy insurance from another party in order to protect itself. So what began as default risk on a single loan became a chain of counterparty risk.

Where there is hedging there is also speculation, so it wasn't long before institutions started placing bets in this market, though if you think about it you can see that the insurer in the transaction described above was placing a bet. It was betting that the company wouldn't default.

Now, this might look like insurance, which is a bet on the part of the insurer that your house won't burn down or your car won't get totaled, but there are important differences. Houses and cars can be grouped by standard categories, and the probabilities of their burning down or being totaled are known, so that insurance companies can price the insurance at rates that will cover their losses and produce profits.

The probabilities of default on car loans and traditional home mortgages are also known, though they're subject to economic conditions that don't have much effect on fires or accidents. But insurance against default risk went far beyond these mundane areas. In fact, it was mostly used in situations for which there wasn't a lot of experience for determining the probability of default, which means that there wasn't a sound basis for pricing such insurance.

Also, credit default swaps differed from futures and other traditional forms of hedging in two very important respects. First, they were mostly customized to fit particular situations. And second, they were traded in an over-the-counter market that had no rules and no system for recording transactions, so they created counterparty risk that could neither be identified nor quantified in ways that would enable anyone to determine who was on the hook for what and for how much.

The problem was, if you had sold large amounts of default risk insurance and later didn't like the way things were going, you couldn't drop out of the game and take your losses as you could in an exchange market. You were stuck in your position, and the only thing you could do about it was to buy insurance from other institutions, passing the risk on to them. But they in turn passed the risk on to other institutions, so no one knew who would end up holding the bag. And meanwhile, driven by the frenzy of selling and buying insurance against default risk, the amount of credit default swaps outstanding in the market soared to a level that was many times the amount of default risk being insured.

7

Bubbles and bursts

You're watching a kid with a wad of bubble gum in his mouth embark on the adventure of blowing a bubble. It starts small but it gets bigger, and it keeps getting bigger until it finally reaches the point where you know it'll burst. For a while it defies the laws of nature, and you can tell that the kid expects *this* bubble to keep getting bigger. But then it bursts, leaving a sticky pink mess on his nose.

Financial bubbles follow this process, except that instead of being filled with air they're filled with money. They start small but they get bigger, and they keep getting bigger, and even after they've reached the point where experience tells us they can't go on, we delude ourselves into thinking that *this* time it's different. This time it'll go on forever.

Too much money

Since we have such a rich language, we can say "blow up" a balloon or "inflate" a balloon. They mean the same thing, and they both imply the use of air to make something bigger. But when we talk about prices getting higher we don't use the word "blowup," we use the word "inflation." Maybe that's because economists (like all specialists) use longer words to explain what's happening.

Inflation is simply a general increase in the prices of the goods and services that are major items in people's budgets. If the price of a box of paper clips goes up but the price of no other item goes up, that's not inflation since paper clips aren't a major item in our budgets. If the price of gasoline goes up, economists wait until they see what happens with the prices of other items, and meanwhile they provide two rates of inflation—one that includes the price of gas and another that doesn't. But when we start paying more for electricity and heating oil and the delivery of items we buy over the internet, we know we have inflation, whatever they tell us.

What causes inflation? The classical answer is too much money chasing too few goods. It's a simple explanation, which has a lot to be said for it.

Suppose there are six kids on a playground. They each have a dollar, and they all want to buy a soda. Along comes a kid with a six-pack of soda, which he bought for three dollars. He wants to make a profit, so he offers to sell his soda for two dollars a can. The six kids tell him they only have one dollar each. The kid with the soda does some quick figuring, and he concludes that if he sells the soda for one dollar a can he'll get six dollars, or three dollars more than he paid for the six-pack, so he sells the soda for a dollar a can.

Now suppose in the same situation the six kids have two dollars each. How much will they pay for a can of soda? They will almost certainly pay two dollars since they're thirsty, they have the money, and the kid with the six-pack is the only game in town. In other words, there's now more money on the playground chasing the same six cans of soda.

So we know what causes inflation—too much money in the system. But do we know where that money comes from? We get it from our wages, salaries, and tips, and our employers get it from their revenues, but that doesn't tell us where the money ultimately comes from.

If you're paying for something with cash, you know where that came from—the government printed it. But if you're paying with a credit card, you may not know exactly where that money came from. You may not even think of your credit card as money, but up to your limit it's as good as cash.

So where did it come from? It came from the government, not directly but through the financial system, mainly through commercial banks. The government decides how much money should be in the system (money supply), and then it takes actions to produce that amount of money.

For example, if the government wants more money in the system it takes actions that increase the capacity of banks to make loans, and in normal times if banks have more capacity to make loans, they make more loans, being motivated by their desire to make more profits. With a higher volume of loans, banks are willing to accept lower interest rates, and with loans available at lower rates, individuals and businesses borrow more and spend more, which helps the economy. That's why the government would decide to put more money into the system—to help the economy.

If people have more money to spend and if the economy has the capacity to produce more goods and services, then having more money in the system won't drive up prices. But suppose at some point the economy runs out of capacity to produce more. What happens to prices? The same thing that happened to the price of soda on the playground. Prices go up, and you have inflation.

Now, when the government implements a policy of "easy money," it always watches for signs of inflation, and when it determines that there is a risk of inflation, it takes actions that decrease the capacity of banks to make loans, which leads to higher interest rates and less borrowing and less spending. Prices respond just as they would if we took away that extra dollar we gave the kids on the playground.

But if there are no signs of inflation, then the government stands back and lets the economy hum along. It follows the policy "If it ain't broke, don't fix it."

Asset bubbles

While the government's keeping an eye on the prices of goods and services it might not notice or care about the prices of assets since they're not included in measures of inflation.

What assets are we talking about? Things in which people invest money such as land, buildings, collectibles, or stocks of companies in particular industries.

Let's follow the process of what happens. Assume there's too much money in the system but there are no signs of inflation, so the government doesn't intervene. And remember that most of the excess money is concentrated in the hands of investors or institutions that represent them. Naturally, they don't want their money to be idle, so they've invested it in Treasury bonds.

But with so much money available to invest in Treasury bonds, the return on these bonds has declined to a level where it's hardly worth investing in them. If you don't understand why, imagine yourself in a position where a hundred banks were eager to lend you money to start your own business. With so much competition among the banks, you would pay a relatively low interest rate on your loan.

Not satisfied with the return they're making on Treasury bonds, investors look for opportunities to make higher returns on their money. They move their money into stocks and into bonds of solid corporations. For a while they're satisfied, but then they realize that they're not earning a higher return than the average investor, so they look around and they discover high-yield bonds. They move a lot of money into these bonds, and other investors follow them.

With more money available for them, companies that never could issue bonds because they were so shaky are now able to issue bonds, so the quality of high-yield bonds declines. And with so much money chasing them the difference (spread) between the interest rates paid by shaky companies and the rates paid by the U.S. Treasury narrows to a point where the return on high-yield bonds isn't justified by their risk. But by then investors, lulled by the fact that there hasn't recently been a default on these bonds, have forgotten how risky they are.

Inevitably, after several defaults the bubble bursts, and investors rush to sell these bonds, but by then it's too late. The "high-yield" bonds have become "junk" bonds, and no one wants to buy them.

The junk-bond bubble occurred in the late 1980s. A more recent bubble, known as the dot-com bubble, occurred in the late 1990s. Investors, who had a lot of excess money, started putting it into companies that had plans to use the internet. The typical business model was to use capital to build an internet network that would eventually become profitable. The money came from venture capital and initial public offerings of stock that were often based on nothing more than a business plan.

With money pouring into the market, the prices of dot-com shares went up, which attracted more money as investors began to assume that the prices of these shares could only go up. At the peak of this bubble new companies were able to sell their stock in the market even though they had no revenues. By then people were buying on speculation.

The collapse of this bubble was triggered in early March of 2000 by a massive sellout of leading high-tech stocks that was followed by a chain reaction of selling. Only two months earlier a dot-com company had acquired the world's largest media company in a transaction rather like the one in which a Dutchman acquired a mansion with a single tulip bulb at the peak of the tulip mania, which occurred in 1637. Investors, suddenly realizing that too much money had been invested in internet companies, pulled their money out of this market, and down went the prices of these stocks.

The bubble process

If we look back at history, we see that a lot of asset bubbles have occurred over the past four hundred years or during the era of modern finance.

These bubbles include the famous South Sea Bubble and the Mississippi Scheme as well as bubbles in commodities, ranging from silver to baseball cards. None of these bubbles was exactly like any other bubble, but they were similar in ways that we can see with hindsight.

- There is excess money in the system.
- The excess money seeks assets that offer higher returns than traditional investments.
- Some investors invest in a promising situation.
- Other investors follow them.
- The price of the asset starts going up.
- Attracted by the price increase, more money flows into the market for the asset.
- The price of the asset goes up further.
- At some point people begin to believe that the price of this asset will go up forever, and even skeptics believe that its price can never go down.
- Something makes people question these beliefs.
- Investors who got into the game early sell the asset and take their profits.
- As the price goes down, investors who bought the asset at the peak lose money. If they borrowed money to buy the asset, they are forced to sell it.
- The price of the asset goes down further.
- Investors who bought the asset with their own money panic and sell it.
- The price of the asset goes down further.
- More investors who borrowed money to buy the asset are forced to sell it, and its price goes down further.
- At some point the price goes into a downward spiral.
- The market for the asset collapses.

A few aspects of the bubble process need special mention. One is the use of borrowed money to buy the asset, or the use of leverage. As the price of the asset goes up, investors borrow money to buy it. That exposes them to the risk of being forced to sell if the price goes down. If you have only your own money at risk, you can stay in the game, but if you have taken loans secured by the asset then you can be forced out of the game. The forced sales by investors who have borrowed money to buy the asset can send its price into a downward spiral, with more investors being forced to sell at every level as the price goes down.

Another aspect that needs special mention is the false sense of security that investors have, based on their belief that the price of the asset will only go up. And even if some of them hedge their risk, they may find that the insurance they bought is worthless.

During the tulip mania investors used futures contracts for hedging and speculating. Buyers of these contracts had to pay transaction fees, but neither party had to put up initial margin or additional margin if prices went against their position, as they do in an exchange market. The counterparty for each of these contracts was an individual, not an exchange, so when the market for tulips collapsed there was nothing of substance to back up the contracts.

On one side people were holding contracts that obligated them to buy tulips at prices that were far higher than the current price in the real market, and on the other side people were holding contracts that entitled them to sell tulips at the higher prices. The people who lost the game were ruined, and the people who won never got paid. If the people who had contracts to sell tulips were hedging their position in tulips, they were out of luck. The insurance they thought protected them turned out to be worthless.

Suppose the government had required futures contracts to be traded on an exchange. When the market crashed, there would have been enough money with the exchange to pay the winners, and the losers would already have taken their losses. So the damage would have been contained.

8

A perfect storm

Perfect storms do not happen every day. They only happen when there are conditions that make them likely to happen, and even then they don't necessarily happen. That's why weather forecasts are so uncertain.

Though meteorologists are often wrong, at least they're always on the lookout for a storm, and they always warn us when they see that a storm is likely to happen. In that respect they're different from the government officials who preside over our financial system. The latter are afraid that if they warn us about a likely economic storm, we'll act in ways that will make such a storm inevitable. If we hoard our money and stop spending, it'll hurt the economy. So even if they see a storm coming, they hope they're wrong and they don't want to upset us, whereas meteorologists always seem to hope they're right and enjoy upsetting us.

Another important difference is that meteorologists don't play any role in making the weather, whereas our government does play a role in driving the financial system. In fact, it plays two main roles: a regulatory role and a monetary role.

In its regulatory role the government protects individuals from bank failure by insuring bank deposits up to a certain amount. And the government examines bank loans to make sure that they meet certain credit standards. So it pays a lot of attention to the traditional activities of commercial banks—taking deposits and making loans.

With respect to financial markets, the government operates on the principle that markets are best left alone, so it tends to intervene only to protect individuals from specific abuses such as fraud and price manipulation. Since individuals are most exposed to such risks in stock markets, the government plays a major role in regulating and supervising these markets.

Until the crash the government paid much less attention to financial markets in which the players are institutions. This policy was based on the assumption that institutions know what they're doing and will act rationally. Now, before you laugh at the government for making such a naïve assumption, remember that traditional economic theory is based on the assumption that people know what they're doing and will act rationally.

The other main role that our government plays in the financial system is to control the amount of money in the system. The Federal Reserve keeps an eye on two sets of indicators—one that tells them if the economy is growing or shrinking, and another that tells them if prices are rising or falling. It tries to prevent the economy from shrinking (recession) and prices from rising (inflation).

It's like when you're driving at night on a winding road with no lights but only a line in the middle and a line on the right to guide you. If you go off course to the right, you may hit a tree, and if you go off course to the left, you may collide with an oncoming car. Understandably, the driver of our economy would rather hit a tree than have a head-on, so it errs on the side of easy money.

Conditions for a storm

When we talked about bubbles we said they start forming when there's excess money. In response to the burst of the dot-com bubble in 2000 the Federal Reserve, mindful of the fact that Japan's economy had suffered a head-on, went out of its way to avoid a recession by making a lot of money available for banks to lend and people to spend.

This excess money was injected into the financial system at a time when the prevailing philosophy was to avoid regulating financial markets and to encourage innovation. It was like putting a fast car with few safety features into the hands of a teenager and letting him go on the open road.

Having put excess money into the system, the Federal Reserve naturally worried about inflation, and it watched for signs of inflation, ready to reverse its policy of easy money. But it didn't see any signs of inflation. In fact, prices were unusually stable in almost every country in the world.

This welcome price stability was mainly due to two factors. First, with the flood of cheap imports from China and other emerging countries, there was downward pressure on prices of manufactured goods. And second, with the abundance of cheap labor in the world, there was downward pressure on wages. So we didn't get into an upward spiral of higher prices, followed by higher wages to compensate workers for higher prices, followed by higher prices to compensate businesses for higher wages, and so on.

To our central bankers it looked as if they could get away with a policy of easy money. They had the benefits of the policy (more spending) without the costs (inflation). When anyone pointed out that this policy caused the recent dot-com bubble and might cause another bubble, the chairman of the Fed (who by then had been in the position too long) argued that it wasn't his job to worry about bubbles, and in any case you couldn't identify a bubble until after it had burst.

In fact, a bubble had already started to form in the housing market, and now the excess money was attracted there. As prices went up, more money was attracted to housing, and it was coming not only from people who wanted a home or a second home but also from people who wanted to speculate in the housing market. Now, even when there are speculators every market sooner or later reaches a point where it begins to run out of potential buyers, and that would have happened with the housing market if a conflux of government policy and private ingenuity hadn't expanded the number of people who could buy a home.

Government policy promoted home ownership on the assumption that homeowners are more solid citizens than renters. Under this policy government-sponsored Fannie Mae and Freddie Mac were encouraged to expand the secondary market for home mortgages. And motivated by higher profits, Fannie and Freddie did what the government wanted.

Private ingenuity provided arguments for bankers to justify lowering the credit standards on mortgage loans so that more people would qualify for them. First, they no longer required a down payment on the grounds that rising prices would build equity in the home for the borrower and the lender. Second, they offered a "teaser" rate, a low initial rate that made it look as if the borrower could pay the mortgage. The borrower got this low rate for only two years, and it would be adjusted, but since the new rate would be based on market rates in the future, no one knew what it would be, and no one could say for sure that it would be higher. And third, the loans could be structured in ways that required the borrower to pay only interest and no principal, again on the grounds that rising prices would build equity in the home. This grace period lasted for only two years, but by then rising incomes would enable borrowers to handle the payments.

Such loans became known as "subprime mortgages" since they were lower in quality than traditional home mortgages. In fact, they met none of the credit standards that banks used to apply to home mortgages. But the bankers who originated these loans were eager to collect the upfront fees, and if they thought about what might happen in the future, they assumed that rising prices would build equity in the homes, so they would be covered.

In any case, the banks had no intention of keeping these loans on their books and bearing the risk of default. They packaged them and issued securities backed by them, slicing them up in a variety of forms so that they could offer different levels of risk and return to investors. The forms that were structured to appear less risky were given the stamp of approval by the firms that rate debt securities for default risk, so they were easy to sell to investors who were looking for ways to earn higher returns on their money.

The entrance of a lot more home buyers drove prices up at the low end of the market. People who had bought homes earlier at that level now had capital gains that enabled them to move up to the next level, which drove prices up at that level, and so on, all the way up to the high end of the market. By then we had a bubble in the making, but the government's policy was not to intervene.

The higher prices at all levels created windfalls for people who had bought homes earlier. They found that they had a lot more equity in their homes than they had anticipated, and they tapped into that equity by increasing their mortgages or taking home equity loans. At the time it didn't seem imprudent to go more deeply into debt since the relationship between their mortgage and the value of their home was about the same as when they had bought it, and they believed that its price would keep going up.

Converting their homes into cash machines enabled many people to spend more than they were earning, and that helped the economy. In fact, the growth and apparent stability of our economy attracted money from countries such as China where people were spending less than they were earning. Ironically, the savings of the frugal Chinese enabled profligate Americans to spend money as if there were no tomorrow. But as long as the prices of their homes kept rising, Americans didn't feel any need to save money. The gains on their homes would provide all the money they would ever need.

Among bankers this false sense of security was enhanced by the fact that they were insuring themselves against default risk with the new methods of hedging that we talked about earlier (credit default swaps). If they were holding loans or debt securities about which they had any doubts, they could buy insurance, and the institutions that sold them insurance could in turn buy insurance from someone else. So in theory the risk of default could be spread to an extent where no one was at risk, which in fact meant that everyone was at risk, and since default insurance was done over the counter, no one knew who the ultimate insurer was, or whether whoever was holding the bag would be good for the money.

The storm

Not surprisingly, the crisis began with subprime mortgages since they were the most vulnerable level of the market, the most exposed to default risk.

Since the housing bubble was unsustainable, as all bubbles are, it didn't take much to turn things in the wrong direction for investors—a leveling of prices in a California suburb, or a rise in defaults on subprime mortgages as teaser rates were replaced by higher market rates. It didn't take much to turn what looked like a virtuous cycle into a vicious cycle.

When the price of an asset involved in a bubble stops going up, the assumption on which the game was based is suddenly in doubt, and when buyers fail to make payments on their contracts, the asset is sold under distress. Defaults on subprime mortgages led to foreclosures and forced sales, which drove down prices, putting more and more borrowers in a position where the amount of their mortgage was greater than the value of their home.

If the negative effects of this vicious cycle had been limited to subprime mortgages it would have been bad enough, but remember how when prices of homes at the low end of the market started going up, they drove up prices of homes in the middle and high ends of the market. If you own a home at the lower level of the middle and you want to sell it, you're competing with a home at the upper level of the low end, so when prices go down at the low end, you have to lower the price for your home in order to sell it.

The price declines in homes varied according to location. Declines in the hot spots were much greater than in the cool spots, but soon we were looking at an average decline of ten percent nationwide, with predictions of an average decline of twenty or even thirty percent by the time the prices finally hit bottom. People who had bought homes at the peak with a ten percent down payment lost all their equity, and people who had bought with nothing down were now underwater.

At first we heard about the people who couldn't pay their mortgages, but then we began to hear that some banks might be in trouble. That was a surprise since we assumed that banks weren't holding the mortgages they had originated but had sold them to investors and spread the risk. And if they were holding any securities that were backed by mortgages, they must have insured the default risk. So how could banks be in trouble?

It turned out that banks had kept some mortgage-backed securities or bought them, in either case borrowing money to finance them. Since the interest rate banks earned on these securities was higher than the rate they paid on the borrowed money, they made a profit simply by carrying these securities. And they believed that the value of these securities would go up, producing an additional profit.

It also turned out that banks had loaned money to buyers of the mortgage-backed securities that they had originated. They had either made these loans directly to the buyers or indirectly by providing the buyers with backup lines for their commercial paper. In other words, the securities went out the back doors of the banks, but the risk of financing them came in the front doors, exposing them to huge potential losses. It makes you wonder if the banks would have abandoned their standards if they had known that they would end up bearing the risk on these securities.

As the default rate on subprime mortgages began to go up, the value of securities backed by these mortgages began to go down. Banks are required to value securities in their portfolios at market prices, so when market prices of securities backed by subprime mortgages went down, banks that had positions in them had to mark them down (mark to market), which produced losses. The only alternative was to sell these securities in the market, which also would have produced losses. And banks preferred "paper" losses to real losses.

Now, remember there are (or were) two kinds of banks: commercial banks, which take deposits and borrow money from the market, and investment banks, which cannot take deposits and therefore have to borrow money. Remember that commercial banks used ten dollars of other people's money (deposits and borrowed money) for every dollar of their own money (capital), while investment banks used twenty or even thirty dollars of other people's money (all borrowed money) for every dollar of their own money. So investment banks not only had less reliable sources of money than commercial banks, they also were more highly leveraged.

The problem came to light when some investment banks reported losses on securities backed by subprime mortgages. Two of these banks began to have trouble borrowing in the market to finance their operations, and they were in danger of becoming illiquid. For a while it looked as if the problem might be limited to investment banks, which were more vulnerable than commercial banks, but as prices in the housing market kept falling, the losses on securities backed by subprime mortgages kept mounting, and when commercial banks reported losses on these securities, it became clear that the problem wasn't limited to investment banks, and it wasn't limited to our country.

What happened then was extraordinary. Over the years we had seen crashes of stock markets, which are easy to follow since they're visible. But this was something we couldn't see since it was happening in markets that are all but invisible to the public. We talked about these markets earlier, the markets in which banks borrow from corporations (bank CDs) and from other banks (Fed funds). We also talked about how investment banks borrow from commercial banks by pledging securities. Well, knowing what they had done themselves, banks began to worry about other banks, and they began to assume the worst. They began to assume that other banks were holding huge amounts of securities backed by subprime mortgages, and that these banks were relying on huge amounts of default risk insurance from institutions that wouldn't be good for the money.

At that point the markets for borrowed money seized. It was like what happens when the engine of your car seizes— everything stops. Since the public couldn't see this happening, they wondered what "credit crunch" meant. It meant that banks had stopped making loans. It meant that banks had stopped lending even to each other.

We saw the crashes of stock markets around the world, and they were bad enough, but we didn't see what was far worse— the crash of the financial system.

9

Government to the rescue

In the movies when people are in serious trouble, someone usually arrives in the nick of time to rescue them. We've seen so many rescues in movies and on television that we expect them in real life. And we expected the government to do something about the crash of the financial system, especially since it happened during an election year.

But our government had no direct experience in dealing with a systemic failure. It had told governments in Asia and Latin America and Eastern Europe what to do when they had a crisis, giving advice that was based on theory, but it's different when the problems are your own—and of your own making. At first, you can't believe what is happening, and then you spend valuable time justifying your prior actions and blaming other people. In this case, the prime suspects were those greedy people on Wall Street.

When you finally realize that instead of just talking about the problem you have to do something about it, you reach for tools you've used in the past. But you quickly find that they don't apply to this situation, so you have to improvise. You have to try something and see if it works. If it doesn't, then you have to try something else.

Too big to fail

Before the crash the government had a lot of experience in dealing with banks that got into trouble. In the early 1980s a number of commercial banks got into trouble, and in the late 1980s a number of savings banks got into trouble. In some cases these banks became illiquid, and in others they became insolvent. In all cases the government applied the same principle. If the bank was too big to fail, then the government saved it, usually by getting a healthy bank to take over the ailing bank, with government support to the extent necessary. For example, the government would remove the worst loans from the books of the ailing bank and assume the risk for them. The healthy bank would then be willing to assume the risk for the remaining loans and assume the liability for the deposits. That spared the government the expense of having to pay depositors out of its insurance fund.

If the bank wasn't too big to fail, then the government would let it fail. How did the government decide that a bank wasn't too big to fail? Usually by its size, but also by the extent to which the financial system depended on it. For example, in the savings and loan crisis the government let a lot of banks fail, and it created a special fund to purchase their loans, which were mostly residential and commercial mortgages. This fund was called the Resolution Trust.

When banks got into trouble this time, the government fell back on the principle it had used before to decide which banks should be saved. But it had to apply the principle to a new situation since the banks that were most obviously in trouble were investment banks, which didn't fall within the normal jurisdiction of the Federal Reserve. So the government was forced to improvise and apply the too-big-to-fail principle not only to investment banks, which it had never done before, but also to an insurance company, which lay even further outside of its normal jurisdiction.

The first government intervention occurred in the middle of March 2008 when the Federal Reserve quickly arranged for Bear Stearns, an investment bank, to be acquired by JPMorgan Chase, a commercial bank. The problems of Bear Stearns had become evident eight months earlier when it reported that two of its hedge funds had lost almost all their value from investments in subprime mortgages. Four months later the firm revealed that it had incurred further losses in mortgage-backed securities, and from then on the news went from bad to worse. It wasn't long before the bank was facing a liquidity problem, meaning that its sources of borrowed money were drying up since potential lenders had growing doubts about the value of its collateral.

While Bear Stearns teetered on the brink of collapse, the government worried about the effects that the failure of a major investment bank would have on financial markets. In particular, the government worried about the transactions for which this bank was the counterparty. If a link in the chain suddenly broke, what repercussions would that have on the system? No one knew, and at that point the government decided not to take any chances. With its support JPMorgan Chase provided an emergency loan to Bear Stearns and then agreed to take it over. To facilitate the acquisition the Federal Reserve assumed the risk on almost $30 billion of Bear Stearns' worst assets. So they used the same approach they had used in previous crises to save commercial banks, except that they saved an investment bank.

The efficient rescue of Bear Stearns appeared to calm the financial markets, but over the next several months the vicious cycle of defaults on mortgages, foreclosures, forced sales, and falling prices in the housing market intensified, and the values of securities backed by mortgages kept falling. By the end of the summer the storm was gathering in full force, and if it had been a hurricane it would have gone off the charts.

We talked earlier about Fannie Mae and Freddie Mac, the government-sponsored but privately-owned companies that make a secondary market for home mortgages by buying them from banks that originate them, packaging them, and issuing securities backed by them to borrow money from investors. They also hold mortgages they have purchased. So Fannie and Freddie operate like investment banks in the sense that they underwrite securities and borrow money from the market to fund their operations.

Investors were willing to make loans to Fannie and Freddie since they had confidence in the mortgages that backed their securities, which conformed to certain guidelines. They also assumed that if Fannie or Freddie got into trouble, they would be rescued by the government. In fact, investors believed that debt securities issued by Fannie and Freddie were implicitly guaranteed by the government, as evidenced by the lower rates they were willing to accept on these securities.

Responding in the late 1990s to the government policy to promote home ownership for low-income families, Fannie and Freddie extended their market-making activities from traditional mortgages to subprime mortgages, which expanded their operations and exposed them to greater risks. By 2008 Fannie and Freddie owned or guaranteed about half of our $12 trillion mortgage market.

During the summer of 2008 investors were worried about Fannie and Freddie, assuming they had to be affected by what was happening in the subprime mortgage market. Those who held shares in these companies sold them, believing that if there was a government bailout stockholders would not be covered, and by August shares of the two companies had fallen by ninety percent from their high. By then lenders were worried about Fannie and Freddie, despite their belief that their loans were implicitly guaranteed by the government. At such times implicit isn't good enough.

In early September, applying the principle of too big to fail, the government took over Fannie Mae and Freddie Mac, and with this action nationalized half of the mortgage market. For that purpose the government had authority to commit up to $800 billion of funding. To put this figure into perspective, remember that the government committed $200 billion to bail out the savings and loans in the late 1980s.

A week later Merrill Lynch, an investment bank, made the headlines. Since the beginning of the year the bank had been reporting losses from its investments in subprime mortgages, quarter after quarter, and by the end of the summer it had lost almost $52 billion in subprime mortgages. Like Bear Stearns, it was facing a severe liquidity crisis, but instead of waiting for a government bailout, Merrill sold itself to Bank of America, a commercial bank, in a deal that would prevent its shareholders from being wiped out.

Lehman Brothers, another investment bank, didn't fare so well. It too was in trouble because of subprime mortgages, and as it reported quarterly losses in 2008 its stock plunged. By late summer Lehman was desperately trying to raise capital, but it wasn't able to make a deal without the government's support. In this case, for reasons that still aren't entirely clear, the government decided not to intervene, and the day after Merrill Lynch announced its deal with Bank of America, Lehman filed for bankruptcy. Perhaps having second thoughts, the Federal Reserve then supported a group of banks in the liquidation of Lehman's assets.

The next day the Federal Reserve intervened to save American International Group (AIG), an insurance company, which was facing a liquidity crisis after a downgrade in its credit rating. AIG was the world's largest insurance company, and it was presumed to be the counterparty on a huge amount of credit default swaps. Instead of finding another institution to acquire AIG, which probably wouldn't have been feasible, the Federal Reserve agreed to lend $85 billion to AIG in return for the right to buy slightly less than eighty percent of its equity. In other words, AIG was nationalized, just as Fannie Mae and Freddie Mac were, except that AIG wasn't a government-sponsored entity. But AIG was too big to fail, and only three weeks later the Federal Reserve provided an additional $38 billion to AIG to make sure it didn't fail.

Saving the system

During that busy September the government used an ad hoc approach to prevent a crash of the whole financial system, focusing on individual banks, deciding if they should be saved, and finding ways of saving them. This approach had been used before, it was more or less within the government's authority, and it bought time.

But it wasn't opening the credit markets, which remained in a state of seizure, and it wasn't restoring trust in the system. So after the rescue of AIG the Secretary of the Treasury asked Congress for authority that would enable the government to use a systemic approach.

The basic idea was for the government to buy illiquid assets of banks in a large enough volume to provide liquidity to the system and restart the flow of credit. It was similar to the idea of the Resolution Trust, which bought illiquid assets from the savings and loans. The main differences were that this idea was broader and its purpose was to save the system, whereas the purpose of the Resolution Trust was to liquidate assets of the savings and loans that been declared insolvent.

The idea was based on the belief that banks were solvent but had temporary liquidity problems that could be resolved by enabling them to turn their illiquid assets into cash. In the long run these assets would be good, but in the short run they were not only useless, they were also toxic. If banks could dispose of them, then lenders would again trust them, and the money would flow.

After much debate and some modifications the plan was approved by Congress, which gave the Treasury $700 billion to work with and at the same time increased the amount of deposit insurance to $250,000 per account. That happened on October 3, and it was supposed to restore confidence in the system. But over the next ten days stock markets around the world plummeted, giving a vote of no confidence in the plan, and the credit markets failed to open up.

In response to the ongoing turmoil, the British government tried another idea—injecting money directly into the banks instead of buying their illiquid assets. That would not only make the banks more liquid, it would also make them more solvent since it would directly increase their capital.

Latching onto that idea, our government announced that it would inject $250 billion directly into banks, using for that purpose some of the money that Congress had authorized. A list of banks that would receive injections appeared in the papers, and it became clear that the government was taking an important ownership position in the banks.

In addition, the government agreed to guarantee the full amounts of money held in transaction accounts by businesses to fund their operating expenses, which for these situations effectively removed the $250,000 limit for deposit insurance. With this guarantee, businesses wouldn't have to worry about losing money if their banks failed.

Beyond the banks the Federal Reserve also intervened in the market for commercial paper (short-term debt securities issued by corporations) by setting up a special purpose vehicle to buy commercial paper directly from eligible companies, meaning that the Fed would lend directly to these companies. The purpose was to restart the flow of credit in the market that provides short-term loans to corporations. The Fed didn't specify the amount of money that it would commit for this purpose, it only said that $1.3 trillion of commercial paper would be eligible.

A few weeks later the Federal Reserve announced that it would support money market mutual funds by buying from them up to $600 billion of "used" bank CDs and commercial paper. The purpose was to provide liquidity for these funds, which would increase their ability to meet redemptions and their willingness to resume lending to banks and corporations by buying new bank CDs and commercial paper.

But stock markets continued to show a lack of confidence in the rescue plan as the Dow Jones average fell by thirty percent from early October to the third week of November. The focal point became Citigroup, whose stock in the middle two weeks of November dropped by sixty-six percent. The government had already injected $25 billion into Citigroup to shore up its capital, but for the markets that wasn't enough. Since Citigroup was too big to fail, the only question was how the government was going to save it. After working over the weekend, the government announced on November 24 that it would inject an additional $20 billion of capital into Citigroup and would absorb ninety percent of the losses on $306 billion of the bank's mortgage-backed securities after Citigroup absorbed the first $29 billion of losses.

The next day the government announced that it would buy up to $600 billion of mortgage-backed securities from Fannie Mae and Freddie Mac, and that it would lend up to $200 billion to holders of securities backed by car loans, credit card loans, student loans, and small business loans. These actions were designed to increase the availability of credit to homebuyers, consumers, students, and small businesses.

In case you haven't been keeping track of the money, so far the government has committed at least $7 trillion dollars in bailouts, loans, and guarantees to save the system. And that may not be the end of it.

10

Aftermath

When a storm has finally passed by, we go to the scene and assess the damage, and we wonder what we can do to make sure that when the next storm comes along, as it inevitably will, it'll do less damage.

In the case of storms we don't talk about preventing them since storms are caused by nature. But in the case of financial crises, which are caused by human beings, we should at least talk about prevention. We might start with the question of what could we have done to prevent this crisis?

The short answer is, we could have stuck with principles that served us well in the past. After seeing the damage caused by the crash of 1929-32, our government established systems that were designed to prevent such damage from occurring again. Believing they couldn't prevent a crash, they focused on mitigating damage, but it turns out that by mitigating damage you can reduce the likelihood of a crash.

For example, by providing insurance on bank deposits so that people wouldn't be hurt by the failure of a bank, the government reduced the likelihood of bank failure since most individuals, knowing they are covered by deposit insurance, don't panic when they hear a rumor about their bank. That prevents banks from becoming illiquid and failing as a result of individuals withdrawing their money in a panic.

Another example is the regulatory system the government established to protect people from fraud and manipulation in the stock market. There is also insurance to protect people from the loss of their shares (though not from the loss of money on their shares). While there will always be the odd scandals in the stock market, individuals have confidence that things are generally above board. That prevents this market from failing as a result of individuals refusing to buy stocks under any circumstances.

So before we talk about what should be done to fix the system, let's assess the damage, and then let's find ways to mitigate the damage that will have the secondary benefit of preventing certain types of failure.

Assessing the damage

As we look around after the storm we see homeowners who were damaged by it, not only people who bought homes they couldn't afford but also people who bought homes they could afford. People who can't pay their mortgages have been losing their homes, but people who *can* pay their mortgages have been losing the equity in their homes that they accumulated through years of saving.

Since equity in homes is a reservoir of savings, people now have much less savings. They're poorer than they were a year ago. The prices of their homes at that time may have been inflated, but they counted on the equity they thought they had in their homes. If they didn't tap into it and spend it, they planned to use it for their retirement. So their wealth and their prospects have been diminished.

We also see people who have lost their jobs because their employers couldn't get credit, or couldn't sell enough of their goods or services, or couldn't survive in an economy that has gone into recession. As things get worse, we're going to see more and more people losing their jobs.

We see people who have lost money in their pension funds. As this sentence is being written stock indices are down about forty percent from their highs, so to the extent that people invested their retirement money in stocks, their prospects have been diminished. People now talk about deferring retirement and figuring out how to survive on less.

We see businesses that are having problems, and we see people who have abandoned their plans to start businesses since they can't get loans.

We see governments at the city and state and federal levels that won't have the revenues they need in order to maintain their current level of services.

In the recession that follows the crash, we'll see the damage done to our economy: unemployment, business failures, and government deficits.

We'll have to work hard to repair this damage, and we'll have to think hard to fix the system.

Fixing the system

In order to mitigate the damage from the housing bubble, we need to stabilize the housing market. It's not enough for the government to buy "toxic" assets from banks. It needs to stop the vicious cycle of home prices falling, borrowers defaulting, banks foreclosing, homes being sold under distress, and prices falling in a downward spiral.

The most effective way to stop this cycle is to aid people who are unable (or unwilling) to pay their mortgages. In some cases, it would be enough to provide a mortgage at a fixed rate of around five percent, payable over thirty years. In other cases, the principal of the loan would have to be reduced to a level where borrowers could make the payments. In all cases, the amount of the loan would not exceed ninety percent of the market value of the home. Since all borrowers would have some equity in their homes, they would have an incentive to pay their mortgages, which would solve the problem of people who are able to pay not paying because their mortgages are greater than the market value of their homes.

In cases where banks made loans that didn't conform to traditional credit standards, they would have to absorb the losses resulting from reductions in the loan amounts, so they wouldn't get off scot-free. In cases where they made loans that did conform to traditional credit standards and the borrower went underwater because of the fall in home prices, the government would absorb the losses. The rationale is that banks should have to pay for irresponsible lending but should not have to pay for irresponsible government policy.

Some people say it's too complicated to refinance all those mortgages because they've been packaged, sliced, diced, and transformed into mortgage-backed securities. But the same thing would have happened when borrowers refinanced under normal conditions, or when they prepaid—the payment of the loan would pass through to the investors, reducing the total principal outstanding, as with any type of bond that's prepaid. So it's not really that complicated.

Going forward, the government should avoid repeating its mistakes and creating conditions for another storm. Bubbles are caused by too much money chasing a particular type of asset, and they become dangerous when too much money is being borrowed to buy the asset. If you buy the asset entirely with your own money, you can never be forced to sell it by a fall in its price, whereas if you buy the asset entirely with borrowed money, you can be forced to sell it by the slightest fall in its price, and when you sell it, you make its price fall further, which forces more people to sell it. That's what makes a bubble burst. So the way to mitigate the damage of bubbles is to limit the extent to which people can borrow money to buy the asset.

Instead of only watching for signs of a general rise in prices, the Federal Reserve should also watch for signs of asset bubbles that could have a significant effect on the economy. It doesn't have to worry about baseball cards, but it does have to worry about bubbles in widely held assets, and when it sees a sign of a bubble (a spike in the price of such an asset), then it should require people to use a greater proportion of their own money to buy the asset. This tool is already used to control the extent to which individuals can borrow money to buy stocks (margin requirement), but its purpose is to protect individuals from getting into positions with stocks where they could lose a lot of money. Its purpose should be broadened to control the growth of asset bubbles and thereby protect the economy from the damage that is caused by such bubbles.

By limiting the use of borrowed money (credit) to buy certain assets, the Federal Reserve could resolve the dilemma it finds itself in when the economy is growing at a healthy rate and there are no signs of a general rise in prices (inflation). In that situation, the Fed may conclude that we don't have too much money in the system, and if it sees an asset bubble (as it did in the case of housing), it may conclude that it's better to ignore the bubble (as it did) because if it took any action, it would have to tighten credit in general, which would cause the whole economy to slow down and even fall into a recession. But by tightening credit selectively, the Fed would avoid the effects of tightening credit in general and limit them to those situations where bubbles are forming. With this approach the Fed could prevent asset bubbles from growing to a point where they damage the economy.

If we apply this policy to housing, we can easily see how it would limit the potential damage from another bubble. And we don't have to be innovative, we can simply go back to the credit standards that served us well in the past.

If people want financing to buy a home, they should have to make a down payment of at least ten percent. The lender should have to verify their income. Their mortgage payments plus property taxes should not exceed a certain percentage of their income. They should have to qualify for a loan whose payments are based on the fixed rate for home mortgages at the time, though within certain restrictions they would then be allowed to have a variable rate.

How do you make sure that home mortgages conform to these standards? You make it illegal to issue securities that are backed by nonconforming mortgages. If a bank wanted to offer such mortgages, it would have to keep them on its books and maintain adequate capital to support them.

We can mitigate the damage to banks from excessive use of other people's money by limiting their degree of leverage. In effect, that has already been done for the two remaining investment banks, Goldman Sachs and Morgan Stanley, by their having converted themselves to commercial banks, which are not allowed to have as high a degree of leverage as investment banks. Beyond that the government should require banks to maintain higher ratios of capital for assets that are riskier. This isn't a new idea, it just hasn't gotten very far. In addition, banks should not be allowed to remove from their balance sheets securities that they are guaranteeing to any extent. They can sell them or they can keep them, but they should not be allowed to pretend they have sold them when in reality they have kept them.

To mitigate the damage done by over-the-counter credit default swaps, the players should create an exchange where these securities are recorded and traded. Buyers and sellers of default insurance would have to put up an initial margin, and when the market went against them they would have to put up additional margin or be closed out and replaced by another counterparty. With this type of market we would know who was insuring what, and we wouldn't have to worry about the counterparty not being good for the money. That would prevent failures of institutions because of their exposure to default insurance.

In general, derivatives should be traded on exchanges. If banks want to customize them, they should be required to maintain adequate capital to support them, just as they should for customized mortgage loans. They can be as ingenious as they want, but not with other people's money.

Some people have blamed the crash on the requirement to adjust (mark to market) the values of the securities that banks are holding. They say that this requirement forced the banks to report losses that then undermined confidence in them. They argue that since these losses were only on paper, the banks shouldn't have had to report them. But the liquidation values of these assets were reflected (and perhaps overstated) by their market prices, so it would have been deceptive not to mark them to market. If anything, there should be more requirements to mark the assets of banks to market. Trust depends on transparency, and the less banks knew about the positions of other banks, the less they trusted them. A loss of trust is what made banks unwilling to lend to each other.

Without a doubt damage was done by the false sense of security provided by credit ratings of debt that turned out to be extremely risky. In retrospect it's clear that the ratings given to some mortgage-backed securities could not have been justified by credit analysis. The ratings business was driven by fees, and the fees were paid by the issuers of the securities. This practice must be stopped, and another source of payment must be found for ratings, perhaps a tax on issues of debt securities. The government should require the credit-rating agencies to follow guidelines that would be established by a commission of professionals, and it should hold them accountable for maintaining standards.

Finally, we should face an unpleasant fact about human nature. When people don't bear the full responsibility of their actions they tend to behave less carefully than they otherwise would. In the financial system people take risks with other people's money that they would never take with their own money. This tendency, which we call "moral hazard," cannot be eliminated, it can only be controlled. When there are large monetary rewards for success, then risk-taking is driven by greed, but it's also restrained by fear—until the players start to believe that they've found a way to eliminate risk or reduce it to a level of no consequence. People always get into trouble when they start to believe they're smarter than the people who got into trouble the last time, when they start to believe that this time it's different.

So we need to regulate the behavior of people who play with other people's money. The lesson of the financial crash is very clear. If our financial system had been more closely regulated, the government wouldn't have had to save it, and we could have used that money (so far at least $7 trillion) to make the world a better place.

INDEX